Winning in the Classroom - Using Bartle's Gaming Styles to Empower Learners

Quick Reads for Busy Educators

Cheryl Angst

Published by Cheryl Angst, 2023.

WINNING IN THE CLASSROOM - USING BARTLE'S GAMING STYLES TO EMPOWER LEARNERS

First edition. April 22, 2023.

Copyright © 2023 Cheryl Angst.

ISBN: 979-8223351702

Written by Cheryl Angst.

Also by Cheryl Angst

Quick Reads for Busy Educators

Gamifying Education - How to Engage and Motivate Students Through Games

Unlocking Gamification - Exploring the Impact and Importance in Education

Winning in the Classroom - Using Bartle's Gaming Styles to Empower Learners

Introduction

GAMIFICATION IS INCREASINGLY being recognized as an effective tool in education. By incorporating game mechanics, educators can create an engaging learning environment that encourages student participation and motivation. However, not all games are created equal, and it is important to understand what makes them work. Richard Bartle's research on gaming types provides a framework for understanding how different players approach games and what motivates them. In this book, we will explore how Bartle's gaming types can be used as a basis for lesson and teaching design.

Bartle's research, conducted in the 1990s, identified four distinct gaming types: achievers, explorers, socializers, and killers. Achievers enjoy setting and achieving goals, explorers like discovering new things and exploring the game world, socializers are motivated by building relationships and interacting with others, and killers enjoy competing and defeating others. These types are not mutually exclusive, and most players exhibit a mix of these motivations.

By understanding the different motivations that drive players, educators can design lessons that cater to these different types. For example, achievers may respond well to a lesson that involves setting goals and achieving milestones, while explorers may benefit from a lesson that encourages them to discover and explore new topics. Socializers may benefit from group activities and collaboration, while killers may respond well to competitive activities.

Designing lessons based on gaming types can also increase engagement and motivation. When students are motivated by their own interests and playstyle, they are more likely to be engaged and invested in the learning process. This can lead to increased participation, better retention of information, and ultimately better learning outcomes.

In this book, we will delve into each gaming type and explore how educators can design lessons that cater to their specific motivations. We will provide practical tips for designing lessons that are engaging, fun, and effective. By the end of this book, educators will have a deeper understanding of how gaming types can be used as a basis for lesson and teaching design, and be equipped with the tools to create a gamified learning environment that is tailored to their students' needs.

Bartle's Research

RICHARD BARTLE, A BRITISH game designer and academic, is widely known for his groundbreaking research on player types and gaming. Bartle's work centers around the idea that different people approach games in different ways and with different motivations.

In his research, he identified four primary types of players based on their preferred gameplay styles and motivations:

Achievers

Achievers are players who are primarily motivated by achieving goals and making progress within the game. They enjoy reaching milestones and achieving high scores, and may spend a lot of time grinding or leveling up their characters to gain an advantage.

Explorers

Explorers, on the other hand, are motivated by discovery and learning. They enjoy exploring the game world, discovering hidden secrets and lore, and experimenting with new mechanics or strategies. They may take a more leisurely approach to the game and prioritize exploration over progression.

Socializers

Socializers are players who are primarily motivated by social interaction and relationships within the game. They enjoy chatting with other players, forming alliances or guilds, and participating in group activities or events. They may spend less time on individual gameplay and more time socializing with other players.

Killers

Killers, or "griefers," are players who enjoy causing disruption and chaos within the game. They may engage in activities like trolling, cheating, or griefing other players for their own entertainment. While not all players fall into this category, Bartle's research suggests that the existence of killers within a game can actually enhance the experience for other players by creating a sense of danger and excitement.

Bartle's research has had a significant impact on the gaming industry and on the way games are designed and marketed. Game designers now consider player types when creating new games or features, and many games offer different play styles to cater to different types of players. Beyond gaming, Bartle's research has also been applied to other areas such as education, marketing, and psychology, where understanding different motivations and preferences is key to designing effective programs and strategies.

Overall, Bartle's research on player types has provided a valuable framework for understanding the different motivations and behaviors of players within games. By recognizing and catering to different player types, game designers can create more engaging and immersive experiences for players, while also opening up new avenues for research and application in related fields.

How do you encourage creativity in the classroom?

    a) Provide clear guidelines and parameters for creative projects

    b) Encourage students to think outside the box and experiment with new ideas

    c) Encourage collaboration and sharing of ideas

    d) Foster a competitive atmosphere that motivates students to be creative

Achievers: Characteristics

ACHIEVERS ARE ONE OF the four gaming types identified by Richard Bartle who are motivated by achieving goals, gaining status, and collecting rewards. Achievers derive satisfaction from progressing through a game and achieving success. They enjoy competition and measuring their accomplishments against other players. Achievers tend to be self-motivated and are often seen as leaders within a game community.

One of the defining characteristics of achievers is their focus on goals. They set themselves targets and take great satisfaction in achieving them. This drive to succeed often makes them willing to put in a lot of time and effort into the game, as they aim to become the best at it. Achievers tend to enjoy games that allow them to progress through levels or ranks, as this provides them with a clear sense of accomplishment.

Achievers also value recognition and status. They are often motivated by the desire to be recognized as the best or most successful player in the game. This drive for recognition can sometimes lead to competitive behavior, as they try to outdo other players and prove their superiority. Achievers may also be motivated by rewards, such as in-game items or titles, as a way of demonstrating their status within the game.

Another important aspect of achievers is their sense of community. While they are often competitive, they also recognize the importance of cooperation and teamwork in achieving their goals. Achievers tend to enjoy games that require collaboration, such as raiding or team-based PvP. They also tend to be active in game forums and social media groups, where they can exchange tips and strategies with other players.

Overall, the characteristics of achievers make them an important gaming type to consider when designing games or gamified learning experiences. By providing clear goals, recognition for achievement, and opportunities for community engagement, designers can create experiences that motivate and engage achievers. Understanding the motivations of this gaming type can also help educators design learning experiences that tap into the same drive for achievement and recognition, creating an engaging and rewarding learning experience.

How do you encourage student participation in class?

    a) Use a rewards-based system to encourage participation

    b) Provide opportunities for hands-on exploration and experimentation

    c) Foster a sense of community and belonging in the classroom

d) Create a competitive atmosphere that motivates students to participate

Achievers: Designing Lessons that Appeal

ACHIEVERS ARE MOTIVATED by gaining recognition and achieving goals. They enjoy overcoming challenges and receiving rewards for their efforts. In order to design lessons that appeal to achievers, it is important to provide clear goals, challenging tasks, and meaningful rewards.

One effective strategy for designing lessons for achievers is to create a clear path to success. This could involve breaking down a larger project into smaller, more manageable tasks with specific deadlines and checkpoints. By providing achievable goals and regular feedback, achievers are more likely to stay motivated and engaged throughout the learning process.

Another strategy is to provide opportunities for competition and recognition. Leaderboards, badges, and certificates can all be effective ways to recognize and reward the accomplishments of achievers. However, it is important to ensure that the recognition is meaningful and reflects genuine achievement, rather than simply participation.

Achievers also tend to value mastery and expertise. Providing opportunities for learners to demonstrate and showcase their knowledge and skills can be a powerful motivator. For example, allowing learners to create a portfolio of their work or present their projects to an audience can provide a sense of accomplishment and recognition.

Finally, it is important to ensure that the tasks and activities provided to achievers are challenging enough to maintain their interest and motivation. This can involve providing choices and opportunities for learners to explore and experiment with new concepts and ideas.

Designing lessons for achievers requires clear goals, challenging tasks, meaningful rewards, opportunities for competition and recognition, opportunities for mastery and expertise, and challenging activities that keep learners engaged and motivated. By understanding the characteristics and motivations of achievers, educators can design lessons that appeal to their strengths and maximize their learning potential.

How do you handle conflicts in the classroom?

a) Apply a set of pre-determined consequences to resolve conflicts

b) Encourage students to express their feelings and work through conflicts together

c) Use conflict as an opportunity to build positive relationships and communication skills

d) Encourage healthy competition and channel conflicts into competitive challenges

Achievers: Providing Effective Feedback

ACHIEVERS IN THE GAMING world are highly motivated by progress, achievements, and reaching new milestones. In the educational context, assessments and feedback are critical tools to keep achievers motivated and engaged in learning. Assessment methods that provide clear criteria and feedback on progress towards learning goals will be highly effective for achievers.

Traditional methods of assessment, such as exams and tests, are often not sufficient to motivate and engage achievers. Instead, assessments that allow for progress tracking, such as performance-based assessments and projects that allow for creativity and innovation, are better suited for this group.

Feedback is also critical for achievers. In order to maximize effectiveness, feedback should be specific and focused on improvement. Achievers tend to thrive on a challenge, so feedback that provides them with clear goals to work towards and guidance on how to achieve them will be highly motivating.

One effective feedback strategy for achievers is to provide them with frequent and immediate feedback. This can be accomplished through self-assessments, peer assessments, or teacher feedback. Feedback that provides positive reinforcement for progress and offers constructive criticism on areas for improvement will keep achievers engaged and motivated.

It is also important to provide achievers with opportunities for growth and advancement. This can be done through offering extension activities, enrichment programs, or honors and advanced courses. Providing achievers with opportunities to challenge themselves and reach new levels of mastery will keep them motivated and engaged in learning.

Overall, assessment and feedback strategies that are tailored to the specific characteristics and motivations of achievers will be the most effective. By offering progress tracking, specific and frequent feedback, and opportunities for growth and advancement, educators can keep achievers engaged and motivated in their learning journey.

For which purpose do you primarily incorporate technology into your teaching?

    a) To enhance traditional teaching methods and materials

    b) To create new and innovative teaching approaches

c) To facilitate collaboration and communication among students

d) To create competitive games and challenges that test student knowledge

Explorers: Characteristics

EXPLORERS ARE THE TYPE of gamer who seeks to discover all the hidden and unexplored areas of the game world. They are driven by the desire to uncover the mysteries and secrets of the game, and they are always seeking new challenges and experiences. Explorers are characterized by their curiosity, their love of discovery, and their willingness to take risks.

One of the defining characteristics of explorers is their love of discovery. They enjoy exploring the game world, uncovering hidden secrets and finding new areas to explore. Explorers are not content to simply follow the main storyline of the game; they want to see everything that the game has to offer.

Explorers also tend to be highly curious individuals. They are interested in learning about the game world and its mechanics, and they enjoy experimenting with different strategies and approaches to the game. They are not afraid to take risks and try new things, even if it means failing a few times along the way.

Another characteristic of explorers is their desire for challenge and novelty. They are always seeking out new experiences and challenges within the game, and they are not satisfied with simply mastering the existing content. They thrive on the sense of accomplishment that comes from overcoming difficult challenges and discovering new things.

Finally, explorers tend to be highly self-directed individuals. They do not rely on external rewards or feedback to motivate them; instead, they are motivated by their own internal drive to explore and discover. They are highly independent and tend to prefer working alone or in small groups, rather than relying on larger social structures.

In order to design lessons that appeal to explorers, educators should focus on creating opportunities for discovery and exploration within the classroom. This might involve creating open-ended assignments that allow students to pursue their own interests and curiosity, or providing opportunities for independent research and experimentation. Educators should also be willing to embrace risk-taking and failure as a natural part of the learning process, and should encourage students to take risks and try new approaches to learning. Finally, educators should be mindful of the importance of challenge and novelty in engaging explorers, and should strive to provide opportunities for students to push their boundaries and test their limits.

How do you prefer to assess student learning?

a) Traditional tests and assignments that measure their mastery of the material

b) Open-ended projects that allow for creativity and exploration

c) Collaborative group work that emphasizes teamwork and communication

d) Competitive games and challenges that test their skills and knowledge

Explorers: Designing Lessons that Appeal

EXPLORERS ARE THE GAMERS who love to explore the game world, discover new things, and experiment with different strategies. They are often motivated by the thrill of discovery and the satisfaction of uncovering hidden secrets. In the context of education, explorers are learners who love to experiment with new ideas, investigate different perspectives, and try out new approaches to problem-solving.

Here are some tips for designing lessons that appeal to explorers:

Create Open-Ended Challenges

Explorers enjoy challenges that allow them to experiment with different strategies and solutions. Instead of providing a step-by-step approach, create open-ended challenges that allow explorers to use their creativity and problem-solving skills.

Encourage Self-Directed Learning

Explorers are often self-motivated and enjoy learning at their own pace. Encourage self-directed learning by providing resources and materials that allow learners to explore topics in-depth and at their own pace.

Foster A Collaborative Learning Environment

Explorers enjoy collaborating with others to share ideas and explore different perspectives. Foster a collaborative learning environment by providing opportunities for learners to work together on projects and assignments.

Provide Opportunities For Discovery

Explorers are motivated by the thrill of discovery. Provide opportunities for learners to discover new ideas and perspectives through hands-on activities, experiments, and real-world applications.

Use Gamification Elements

Gamification elements like leaderboards, badges, and rewards can appeal to the explorer's desire for discovery and experimentation. Use gamification elements to encourage learners to explore different topics and take on new challenges.

By designing lessons that appeal to explorers, educators can help learners develop a sense of curiosity and a passion for discovery. Encouraging exploration and experimentation can lead to a deeper understanding of the subject matter and the development of valuable problem-solving skills.

How do you prefer to deliver feedback to your students?

a) Constructive criticism and specific areas for improvement

b) Encouragement and praise for creative thinking and exploration

c) Personalized and individualized feedback that addresses their unique needs

d) Friendly competition and recognition for exceptional performance

Explorers: Fostering Curiosity and Exploration in the Classroom

CURIOSITY AND EXPLORATION are crucial elements in learning, yet they are often undervalued or neglected in traditional classrooms. In this chapter, we will explore how to foster curiosity and exploration in the classroom and how these practices can benefit students' learning and engagement.

Curiosity and exploration are natural instincts that drive our desire to learn and discover new things. However, in traditional classrooms, the focus is often on providing students with answers rather than encouraging them to ask questions and explore on their own. To foster curiosity and exploration, teachers should create an environment that encourages questioning, investigation, and experimentation.

One of the most effective ways to foster curiosity and exploration is by encouraging students to ask questions and investigate topics that interest them. Teachers can provide students with open-ended questions and challenges that encourage them to think critically and creatively. Additionally, teachers can facilitate discussions that encourage students to share their ideas, ask questions, and engage in collaborative problem-solving.

Hands-on learning experiences can help to foster curiosity and exploration by providing students with opportunities to engage in active learning and problem-solving. Teachers can incorporate experiments, simulations, and projects into their lessons to provide students with opportunities to explore and discover on their own.

To foster curiosity and exploration, it's important to create a safe and supportive learning environment where students feel comfortable taking risks and making mistakes. Teachers can encourage risk-taking by providing students with opportunities to try new things and experiment without fear of failure. Additionally, teachers can provide constructive feedback that encourages students to learn from their mistakes and improve their skills.

Fostering curiosity and exploration in the classroom is crucial for promoting student engagement, critical thinking, and problem-solving skills. By creating a supportive learning environment, encouraging questioning and investigation, and incorporating hands-on learning experiences, teachers can help to spark students' natural curiosity and love of learning.

How do you typically respond to students who are struggling with material?

a) Provide extra resources and support to help them catch up

b) Encourage them to explore alternative approaches to learning

c) Create opportunities for them to work with and learn from their peers

d) Set up a friendly competition to motivate them to work harder

Socializers: Characteristics

SOCIALIZERS ARE THE third of four types of gamers identified by Richard Bartle's research on player types. They derive their enjoyment from the social aspects of gaming, such as building and maintaining relationships with other players. Socializers enjoy interacting with others and tend to prioritize collaboration over competition.

One of the key characteristics of socializers is their desire to form connections with other people. They often enjoy the feeling of being part of a community and derive satisfaction from helping others. This trait is reflected in their gaming behavior, as socializers often seek out opportunities to work together with other players and engage in cooperative gameplay.

Another important characteristic of socializers is their preference for communication and social interaction. They enjoy chatting and exchanging ideas with other players, and they tend to value the social aspects of gaming more than the game itself. Socializers also tend to be more interested in the storyline and narrative of games, as this provides them with a sense of immersion and social context.

Socializers are often drawn to games that have strong social components, such as massively multiplayer online role-playing games (MMORPGs) or social simulation games. They tend to be less interested in games that focus on individual achievement or require extensive amounts of solo play. Socializers may also seek out opportunities to engage with other players outside of the game, such as through online forums or social media.

In the classroom, socializers may benefit from group work and collaborative activities that allow them to interact with their peers. They may also enjoy opportunities to engage in discussions or debates, as this provides them with an opportunity to connect with others and share their ideas. Teachers can also foster socialization by creating a positive classroom environment that encourages open communication and collaboration.

Overall, understanding the characteristics of socializers can help teachers design more engaging and effective lessons that foster socialization and collaboration. By recognizing the importance of social interaction and communication, teachers can create a more inclusive and supportive classroom environment that benefits all students.

In a classroom setting, when are you most engaged?

a) When there are clear objectives and a structured lesson plan

b) When creativity and experimentation is encouraged

c) When someone facilitates group work and discussion

d) When competition or gamification elements are incorporated into the learning

Socializers: Designing Lessons that Appeal

SOCIALIZERS ARE THE players who enjoy socializing and interacting with others. They often form communities, make friends, and participate in group activities. In the classroom, these students value collaboration, communication, and relationships with others.

Here are some strategies that can help in designing lessons that appeal to socializers:

Group Projects

Socializers thrive in group settings where they can interact and collaborate with others. Incorporating group projects or activities in lessons can be an effective way to engage these learners.

Role-Playing Exercises

Role-playing exercises can be an excellent way to foster collaboration and communication skills among socializers. It allows them to interact with others in a fun and engaging way.

Peer-To-Peer Feedback

Socializers value feedback and enjoy the opportunity to give and receive feedback from their peers. Incorporating peer-to-peer feedback can create a supportive environment where socializers can learn and grow together.

Interactive Discussions

Interactive discussions can be a powerful way to engage socializers in the learning process. These discussions allow them to express their thoughts and ideas, learn from others, and build relationships with classmates.

Online Platforms

Socializers often use social media and other online platforms to connect with others. Teachers can use these platforms to create online communities or discussion boards that allow socializers to connect with their peers and participate in discussions outside of the classroom.

By incorporating these strategies, teachers can create an environment that fosters collaboration, communication, and relationships with others. It can lead to a more engaging and fulfilling learning experience for socializers, ultimately improving their academic performance and satisfaction.

When working with a group, what are you most likely to do?

a) Take charge and delegate tasks

b) Offer creative ideas and solutions

c) Keep everyone on task and ensure everyone is heard

d) Push for the project to be the best it can be

Socializers: Managing Group Dynamics and Assessing Group Work

GROUP WORK IS A CRITICAL aspect of teaching and learning, and it is essential to manage group dynamics effectively to create a positive learning environment. Socializers are individuals who thrive in social situations and prefer to work collaboratively with others. They are often the glue that holds a group together, and their positive attitudes can help to create a supportive environment for learning. However, socializers can also be easily distracted and may need guidance to stay on task.

To manage group dynamics, teachers must establish clear expectations for group work and set ground rules to ensure that everyone understands their roles and responsibilities. This can help to prevent conflict and ensure that everyone is working towards the same goal. Teachers should also monitor group work closely and provide guidance and support where necessary. Encouraging open communication and fostering a supportive learning environment can also help to promote positive group dynamics.

Assessing group work can be challenging, but it is important to ensure that everyone is contributing equally. Teachers can use a variety of assessment methods, including peer evaluation and self-assessment, to ensure that everyone is accountable for their contributions. Teachers should also provide feedback to students on their group work, highlighting areas of strength and identifying areas for improvement. This can help to reinforce positive behaviors and promote the development of essential teamwork and collaboration skills.

Finally, it is essential to recognize that every student is unique and may have different learning needs. Teachers should be prepared to modify their approach to group work to meet the needs of individual students. This may involve adjusting the group size or composition, providing additional support to struggling students, or providing extension activities for more advanced students.

Managing group dynamics and assessing group work requires careful planning and attention to detail. Teachers must be prepared to establish clear expectations, monitor group work closely, and provide guidance and support where necessary. By fostering positive group dynamics and promoting the development of essential teamwork and collaboration skills, teachers can create a supportive learning environment that enables all students to succeed.

What do you prefer to do with your free time?

a) Set goals and work to achieve them

b) Explore new hobbies or interests

c) Spend time with friends and family

d) Play games that involve competition or strategy

Killers: Characteristics

THE KILLER GAMING TYPE is characterized by a competitive and aggressive nature. Killers thrive on the challenge of beating other players and gaining dominance in the game world. They enjoy conflict and will go to great lengths to achieve their goals, including manipulating other players and exploiting game mechanics.

Killers are often seen as disruptive and can create a negative experience for other players. They enjoy causing chaos and will often act in ways that break the rules of the game. However, they are also highly motivated and can be valuable assets in team-based games, as long as their competitive nature is channeled appropriately.

To appeal to the killer gaming type in lesson and teaching design, it is important to provide opportunities for competition and challenge. Group projects with clear objectives and a competitive element can be effective in engaging killers. However, it is important to ensure that the competitive element is healthy and does not turn into bullying or exclusion of other students.

Assessing and giving feedback to killers can be challenging, as they may not respond well to criticism or negative feedback. Instead, it is important to focus on their strengths and provide opportunities for them to use their competitive nature in a positive way. Acknowledging their achievements and recognizing their successes can help motivate them and keep them engaged in the learning process.

In group work, it is important to manage the dynamics between killers and other students. Encouraging collaboration and teamwork can help channel their competitive nature in a positive direction. However, it is also important to set clear guidelines and consequences for inappropriate behavior, to ensure that the classroom remains a safe and supportive environment for all students.

What is your attitude towards risk-taking in the classroom?

a) Avoid risk-taking and stick to proven methods

b) Encourage students to take risks and try new things

c) Value emotional safety and avoid situations where students may feel uncomfortable

d) Use risk-taking as a motivator and encourage students to embrace challenges

Killers: Designing Lessons that Appeal

DESIGNING LESSONS THAT appeal to the killer gaming type can be challenging as this type of player enjoys competition and prefers to be in a dominant position. Lessons that promote collaboration and teamwork may not appeal to them as much. However, by understanding the characteristics of the killer gaming type, teachers can design lessons that engage and motivate them.

One way to appeal to killers is to introduce competitive elements into the lesson. For example, teachers can create games or challenges where students compete against each other or against the teacher. The key is to create a level playing field where each student has an equal chance to succeed. This can be achieved by setting clear rules and objectives and ensuring that the challenges are fair and balanced.

Another way to appeal to killers is to provide them with opportunities to demonstrate their knowledge and skills. Teachers can assign tasks or projects that allow killers to showcase their abilities and outperform their peers. This can be done by providing extra credit or recognition for outstanding performance, which can motivate killers to strive for excellence.

In addition, teachers can incorporate elements of risk and uncertainty into the lesson to appeal to killers. This can be done by providing opportunities for students to take calculated risks, such as presenting their work to the class or participating in debates. By creating an environment where students are encouraged to take risks, teachers can help killers develop their confidence and take ownership of their learning.

Finally, it is important to create a classroom culture where killers feel valued and respected. Teachers can do this by recognizing and celebrating their contributions to the class. This can be done by providing them with leadership roles or opportunities to mentor their peers. By acknowledging their strengths and abilities, teachers can help killers feel valued and appreciated, which can motivate them to engage more fully in the learning process.

Designing lessons that appeal to killers requires an understanding of their competitive nature and a willingness to provide them with opportunities to demonstrate their skills and knowledge. By incorporating elements of competition, risk, and uncertainty into the lesson, teachers can create an engaging and motivating learning environment for killers.

What kind of professional development opportunities do you find most engaging?

a) Workshops and training sessions that focus on improving teaching skills and classroom management

b) Conferences and seminars that introduce new and innovative teaching approaches

c) Networking events and opportunities to connect with other educators

d) Competitions and challenges that test teaching skills and knowledge

Killers: Creating Healthy Competition and Avoiding Negative Behaviours

WHILE COMPETITION CAN be motivating and enjoyable, it can also lead to negative behaviors and a toxic learning environment. As such, it's important to foster healthy competition in the classroom while discouraging negative behaviors.

One effective strategy for fostering healthy competition is to establish clear rules and expectations for behavior during competitive activities. Teachers can communicate the importance of fair play and sportsmanship and establish consequences for negative behaviors like cheating or bullying. Additionally, teachers can create opportunities for students to practice positive behaviors like congratulating opponents and collaborating with teammates.

Another strategy is to provide opportunities for students to reflect on their behavior and performance during competitive activities. Teachers can ask students to consider how their actions impact others and reflect on areas where they can improve. This can help students develop self-awareness and empathy, leading to a more positive learning environment.

It's also important to encourage collaboration and teamwork during competitive activities. Teachers can create opportunities for students to work together to achieve a common goal, emphasizing the importance of supporting one another and working toward a shared objective. This can help students see the benefits of collaboration and diminish the desire to win at all costs.

Finally, teachers can incorporate non-competitive activities into the classroom to promote a more balanced approach to learning. By emphasizing the value of individual growth and development, rather than just winning, students can learn to appreciate the process of learning and the skills they develop along the way.

Fostering healthy competition and avoiding negative behaviors requires a proactive and intentional approach. By establishing clear expectations, encouraging reflection and collaboration, and promoting a balanced approach to learning, teachers can create a positive and supportive learning environment where students can thrive.

When faced with a difficult problem, what do you do?

   a) Keep working at it until I find a solution

   b) Experiment with different solutions and approaches

c) Discuss it with others to get new ideas and perspectives

d) Look for a way to come out on top, even if it means competing with others

Blending Types: Overlapping and Intersecting

AS DISCUSSED IN PREVIOUS chapters, in Richard Bartle's research, players are classified into four gaming types: achievers, explorers, socializers, and killers. However, in real-world situations, players often exhibit traits from multiple gaming types. Here we will discuss how these gaming types can interact and overlap.

Achievers, for example, may be driven by competition and may exhibit killer traits. They may strive to be the best at what they do and may engage in competition with their peers to achieve that status. Explorers, on the other hand, may have a drive to discover and learn new things and may exhibit traits from all gaming types. They may compete to be the first to discover new information or complete a task, or they may collaborate with others to achieve their goals.

Socializers may also exhibit traits from other gaming types, such as the desire to achieve status and recognition for their social skills, similar to achievers. They may also engage in competition with others to be the most popular or well-liked in a group. Additionally, socializers may collaborate with others to form social bonds and create a sense of community.

Killers, while often seen as the opposite of socializers, may also exhibit social traits. They may form alliances with others to achieve their goals, such as taking down a common enemy or dominating a competition. They may also compete with others to be the most feared or respected player.

Understanding how these gaming types can overlap and interact is important in designing lessons and activities that appeal to a variety of students. Teachers can use this knowledge to create activities that engage multiple gaming types, such as team-based competitions that appeal to achievers and killers, or open-ended exploration activities that appeal to explorers and socializers.

By incorporating elements from multiple gaming types, teachers can create a dynamic and engaging learning environment that caters to the diverse needs and interests of their students. Additionally, understanding how these gaming types interact can help teachers to better manage group dynamics and create a more harmonious classroom environment.

When given a new task, what do you typically do?

a) Break it down into smaller parts and work through it systematically

b) Explore different ways to approach it before settling on one

c) Collaborate with others to brainstorm ideas

d) Find ways to make it more challenging or competitive

Blending Types: Designing Lessons that Appeal

INCORPORATING ELEMENTS that appeal to multiple gaming types can enhance engagement and motivation in the classroom. In this chapter, we will explore how to design lessons that appeal to more than one gaming type.

First, consider the characteristics of the different gaming types and identify areas of overlap. For example, both achievers and explorers may be drawn to challenges, while socializers and killers may be motivated by interactions with others. By identifying these commonalities, you can design activities that appeal to multiple types.

Next, consider the game mechanics that are most appealing to each gaming type. Achievers may enjoy activities with clear goals and rewards, while explorers may prefer open-ended activities that allow for creative problem-solving. Socializers may enjoy collaborative activities and role-playing, while killers may enjoy competitive activities with opportunities to strategize and outmaneuver others.

When designing activities, consider incorporating multiple mechanics that appeal to different gaming types. For example, a scavenger hunt could appeal to both achievers and explorers by providing a clear goal with opportunities for creative problem-solving. Adding in social elements, such as team collaboration, could also appeal to socializers.

It's important to note that not all activities will appeal to every gaming type, and that's okay. It's also important to avoid creating activities that cater exclusively to one type, as this could lead to disengagement and exclusion of other students. Instead, aim to create activities that offer something for everyone, while also providing opportunities for students to explore their individual strengths and preferences.

Finally, be open to feedback from your students. Ask them what they enjoyed about the activity and what could be improved. This will help you better understand the needs and preferences of your students and allow you to continue to design activities that appeal to multiple gaming types.

By designing activities that appeal to multiple gaming types, you can create a more engaging and motivating classroom environment for all students.

When it comes to classroom management, what is your go-to approach?

a) Create a structured and organized classroom environment

b) Allow for some flexibility and autonomy in student behavior

c) Foster a sense of community and belonging through positive relationships

d) Establish clear rules and consequences for negative behavior

Blending Types: Assessing and Meeting the Needs of Diverse Learners

INCORPORATING GAMING elements in the classroom can appeal to a diverse range of learners, including achievers, explorers, socializers, and killers. However, designing lessons that cater to multiple gaming types can be challenging. The key is to strike a balance between the different types while keeping the learning objectives in mind.

One effective approach is to design activities that allow learners to choose their own paths and goals. This gives achievers the opportunity to aim for specific targets, while explorers can explore different possibilities and socializers can collaborate with their peers. Killers can also benefit from such activities as they can compete with others in a healthy and constructive way.

Another strategy is to incorporate game mechanics that appeal to multiple gaming types. For instance, an activity that offers both individual and group rewards can motivate both achievers and socializers. Similarly, a problem-solving activity that requires collaboration can appeal to both explorers and socializers.

Assessment is also a critical component of meeting the needs of multiple gaming types. While traditional assessments such as tests and quizzes may work for achievers, explorers may prefer projects that allow them to explore and experiment, and socializers may thrive in group-based assessments. Killers, on the other hand, may benefit from assessments that allow them to compete with others.

In addition to designing activities and assessments, it is important to provide opportunities for learners to reflect on their learning and provide feedback. This can help them understand their strengths and weaknesses as learners and also help the teacher adjust instruction and activities to better meet the needs of different gaming types.

By keeping the needs and preferences of multiple gaming types in mind, teachers can design lessons that are engaging, challenging, and effective for all learners.

When it comes to lesson planning, what is your primary focus?

a) Ensure that all required material is covered and students are prepared for assessments

b) Provide opportunities for exploration and discovery

c) Create lessons that are engaging and interactive for all students

*d) Incorporate friendly competition and challenges into the
lesson*

Bartle In Practice: High School

IN A HIGH SCHOOL HISTORY class, the teacher decided to implement Bartle's gaming types as a basis for lesson and teaching design. She began by introducing the four gaming types to her students and asked them to complete a survey to determine which type they identified with the most. The majority of the students identified as achievers, but there were also a significant number of socializers and explorers, with only a few identifying as killers.

The teacher used this information to design her lessons in a way that would appeal to each type. For the achievers, she created clear goals and objectives for each lesson and provided a point system to track progress. For the socializers, she incorporated group work and encouraged social interaction during class activities. For the explorers, she included hands-on projects and encouraged independent research. For the killers, she fostered healthy competition through debate-style discussions and mock trials.

One of the benefits of using Bartle's gaming types in the classroom was an increase in student engagement and motivation. Students felt that the lessons were tailored to their interests and learning styles, which helped them to stay focused and interested in the material. They also enjoyed the healthy competition and social interaction that was incorporated into the lessons.

However, there were also some drawbacks to this approach. For example, some students felt that they were not accurately represented by any one gaming type and felt left out of certain activities. Additionally, some students found the point system to be too rigid and felt that it didn't accurately reflect their understanding of the material.

Overall, the teacher felt that using Bartle's gaming types as a basis for lesson and teaching design was a successful approach. By catering to the different needs and interests of each gaming type, she was able to create a more engaging and effective learning environment for her students. However, she also recognized that this approach may not work for every student and that it was important to be flexible and adaptable in her teaching methods.

When learning a new subject, what do you find most helpful?

a) Following a structured outline or course

b) Experimenting with different ways to understand the material

c) Discussing the subject with others and collaborating on projects

d) Looking for ways to challenge myself against others in the subject

Bartle In Practice: Middle School

IN A MIDDLE SCHOOL classroom, the teacher noticed that students had different motivations and preferences when it came to learning. Some students were competitive, while others were more collaborative. This led the teacher to explore the use of Bartle's gaming types as a way to better engage students in the classroom.

The teacher started by identifying the different gaming types that were present in the classroom. Through observation and conversations with students, the teacher identified achievers, explorers, and socializers. The teacher also noticed a few students who displayed characteristics of the killer type.

To design lessons that appealed to these different gaming types, the teacher incorporated different activities and approaches. For achievers, the teacher provided clear goals and objectives and offered rewards and recognition for meeting them. For explorers, the teacher encouraged inquiry and curiosity by allowing students to pursue their own interests and questions. For socializers, the teacher created opportunities for collaboration and group work.

The teacher also made a conscious effort to foster healthy competition and avoid negative behaviors with the few students who displayed characteristics of the killer type. The teacher emphasized the importance of respecting others and encouraged students to compete in a positive and constructive manner.

Overall, the use of Bartle's gaming types in the classroom had several benefits. Students were more engaged in their learning, and the teacher was able to better meet their individual needs and preferences. The teacher also observed increased collaboration and communication among students, and a stronger sense of community in the classroom.

However, there were also some drawbacks to this approach. The teacher found that designing lessons that appealed to multiple gaming types could be challenging and time-consuming. Additionally, the teacher had to be mindful of not reinforcing stereotypes or pigeonholing students into certain categories.

In conclusion, the use of Bartle's gaming types can be a valuable tool for engaging and meeting the needs of diverse learners in the classroom. However, it requires careful consideration and planning to ensure that all students feel seen and valued.

What do you value most in a learning environment?

    a) Clear objectives and specific goals

b) Opportunities for exploration and experimentation

c) Collaborative work and social connection

d) Challenging materials that push me to excel

Bartle In Practice: Elementary School

IN AN ELEMENTARY SCHOOL classroom, the teacher implemented Bartle's gaming types as a basis for lesson and teaching design. The teacher used a variety of approaches to appeal to the different gaming types. To engage the achievers, the teacher created a points system where students received points for completing tasks and achieving goals. For the explorers, the teacher provided opportunities for hands-on activities and encouraged students to ask questions and seek out information. The socializers were given opportunities to work collaboratively in groups, and the killers were given opportunities to engage in healthy competition, such as spelling bees or math challenges.

The benefits of using Bartle's gaming types in the classroom were significant. Students were more engaged and motivated to participate in class activities. They were more willing to take risks and explore new concepts. Students who might have otherwise been disengaged or uninterested in class became more involved and excited about learning. Students were also more willing to work collaboratively and support each other in their learning. Additionally, the teacher was able to more effectively assess students' strengths and weaknesses and tailor instruction accordingly.

However, there were also some challenges with this approach. The teacher found it challenging to balance the needs of the different gaming types and ensure that each type was receiving adequate attention. The teacher also had to be careful not to rely too heavily on one type of activity or lesson, as this could lead to students feeling left out or disengaged. Additionally, some students struggled with the competitive aspects of the class, particularly the killers, and needed extra support and guidance to participate in a healthy and productive way.

Overall, the use of Bartle's gaming types in the elementary school classroom proved to be an effective approach to teaching and learning. The teacher was able to create a more engaging and dynamic classroom environment, and students were more motivated and excited about learning. While there were some challenges associated with this approach, the benefits far outweighed the drawbacks, and the teacher plans to continue using this approach in the future.

When planning a lesson, what motivates you the most?

a) Seeing my students succeed and achieve their goals

b) Discovering new and innovative ways to teach material

c) Collaborating with other teachers to create an engaging and interactive lesson

d) Competing with myself to make the lesson better than the last

Bartle In Practice: Summary

AFTER ANALYZING THE case studies, it is clear that using Bartle's gaming types as a basis for lesson and teaching design can have many benefits, such as increased engagement, motivation, and personalized learning. However, there are also some potential drawbacks that need to be addressed.

One of the main concerns raised in the case studies was the difficulty in meeting the needs of multiple gaming types in a single classroom. This can be solved by designing lessons that appeal to multiple types of learners and providing different options for learning and assessment.

Teachers can also encourage students to work together in groups and collaborate on projects that cater to different gaming types.

Another challenge was ensuring that students do not become too focused on individual achievement and competition at the expense of group learning and social skills. To address this, teachers can incorporate cooperative learning activities and emphasize the importance of teamwork and communication skills. Additionally, they can use incentives that reward positive behaviors and discourage negative behaviors.

Overall, the case studies demonstrate that using Bartle's gaming types as a basis for lesson and teaching design can be a powerful tool for creating a more engaging and effective learning environment. By being aware of potential drawbacks and implementing strategies to address them, teachers can successfully integrate gaming elements into their classrooms to meet the diverse needs of their students.

What kind of games do you most prefer?

a) Ones that have clear objectives and a sense of progression

b) Ones that allow for exploration and discovery

c) Ones that involve playing with friends or meeting new people

d) Ones that are competitive and involve strategy

Determining Player Types

TO DETERMINE THE GAMING types of students in the class, teachers can use a variety of techniques, including observation, student surveys, and assessments. By understanding the gaming types of their students, teachers can better design lessons and activities that appeal to their individual learning preferences.

Observation can be a useful tool for identifying student gaming types. By observing students during group work or independent activities, teachers can note their preferences for social interaction, exploration, competition, or achievement. Teachers can also observe how students react to various types of games or challenges and use that information to infer their gaming types.

Another method for determining student gaming types is to use a survey. There are many online surveys that can be used, such as the Bartle Test of Gamer Psychology[1], which is based on Bartle's gaming types. The survey consists of questions that ask about the individual's gaming habits and preferences, as well as their motivations for playing games. Teachers can also create a simple survey of their own that asks students about their preferences for different types of games and activities, such as socializing, exploring, achieving goals, or competing with others. The survey can also ask about specific games or gaming platforms that students enjoy and how they like to interact with others during gameplay.

Assessments can also be used to determine student gaming types. There are a variety of online assessments available that can provide insight into a student's gaming preferences and tendencies. These assessments often provide detailed reports that can help teachers understand their students' strengths and weaknesses when it comes to gaming.

Quick and Easy Student Survey

A quick way to get an idea of your students' gaming styles is to create a multiple choice survey where the answers to each question reflect an aspect of one of the four gaming styles. In the ten questions below, each "a" answer is an achiever trait, each "b" is an explorer trait, and so on.

When complete, simply tally up the number of "a", "b", "c", and "d" responses to determine a student's predominant gaming style.

WHEN PLAYING GAMES, what type of goal do you find most satisfying?

---

1. http://matthewbarr.co.uk/bartle/

a) Achieving a high score

b) Exploring new areas

c) Completing challenges

d) Competing against others

WHEN PLAYING WITH OTHERS, what do you enjoy most?

a) Being the leader

b) Helping others

c) Being part of a team

d) Winning against others

HOW DO YOU FEEL ABOUT games with a lot of rules?

a) I enjoy learning and following rules

b) I find them boring and sometimes frustrating

c) It depends on the game

d) I prefer games with a few simple rules

WHAT TYPE OF GAME ENVIRONMENT do you prefer?

a) A challenging environment

b) An exploratory environment

c) A collaborative environment

d) A competitive environment

WHEN PLAYING GAMES, what motivates you?

a) Achieving goals

b) Exploring new possibilities

c) Gaining recognition

d) Winning against others

WHEN PLAYING GAMES, what type of strategy do you prefer?

a) Planning carefully to avoid risks

b) Trying out new strategies

c) Taking risks for big rewards

d) Analyzing opponents to gain an advantage

WHAT DO YOU ENJOY MOST about games?

a) The sense of accomplishment

b) The exploration

c) The social interaction

d) The competition

WHAT DO YOU FIND MOST challenging about games?

a) Mastering difficult skills

b) Figuring out new systems

c) Working with others

d) Winning against tough opponents

WHAT TYPE OF GAME REWARD do you find most satisfying?

a) Points or score

b) New items or gear

c) Unlocked achievements or badges

d) Recognition from others

HOW DO YOU APPROACH new games?

a) I read the rules carefully before playing

b) I explore the game world before setting goals

c) I jump in and try things out

d) I analyze the game mechanics before making decisions

For a free PDF copy of this survey (along with a scoring guide) click here[2].

Scoring multiple-choice survey questions to determine a student's gaming type depends on the specific questions used and the scoring system chosen. One possible scoring system is to assign a point value to each response, with responses that align with a certain gaming type receiving higher point values. For example, a question designed to assess a student's preference for socializing in games might assign higher points to responses that indicate a desire to play with others, while a question designed to assess a student's preference for exploration might assign higher points to responses that indicate a desire to explore new areas of a game.

Once all questions are scored, the total point value for each gaming type can be calculated, and the gaming type with the highest score can be determined to be the student's dominant gaming type. It's important to note that this type of survey is not a definitive measure of a student's gaming type, as individual preferences and behaviors can vary widely even within a single gaming type. However, it can be a useful tool for gaining a general understanding of a student's gaming preferences and designing lessons that appeal to their interests.

The author uses the Bartle Test of Gamer Psychology with her students and then imports the data into a spreadsheet for analysis. Using the data, the author is able to create gaming style learner profiles for each student, such as the ones that follow.

---

2. https://drive.google.com/file/d/16-PUk66Z8xtFIKi1uhKCHW2akVafkGYU/
  view?usp=sharing

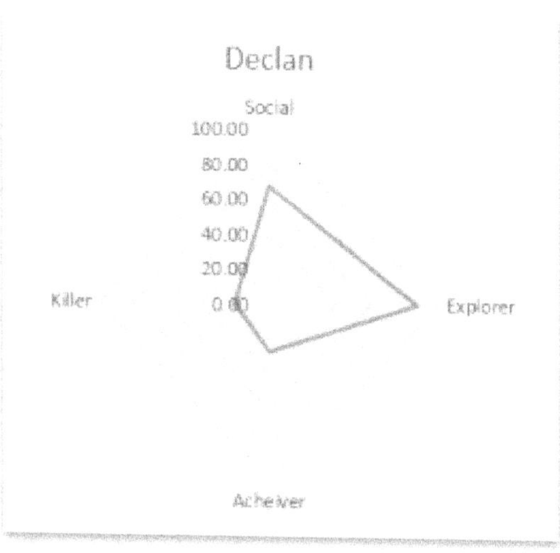
Declan
Social
100.00
80.00
60.00
40.00
20.00
0.00
Killer
Explorer
Acheiver

Francis
Social
100.00
80.00
60.00
40.00
20.00
0.00
Killer
Explorer
Acheiver

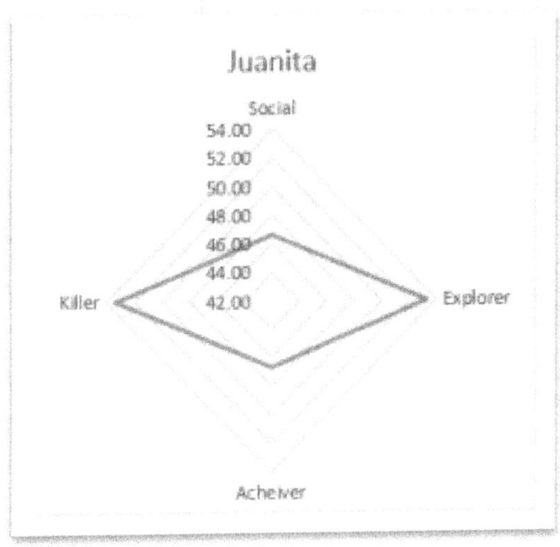

Juanita
Social
54.00
52.00
50.00
48.00
46.00
44.00
42.00
Killer
Explorer
Acheiver

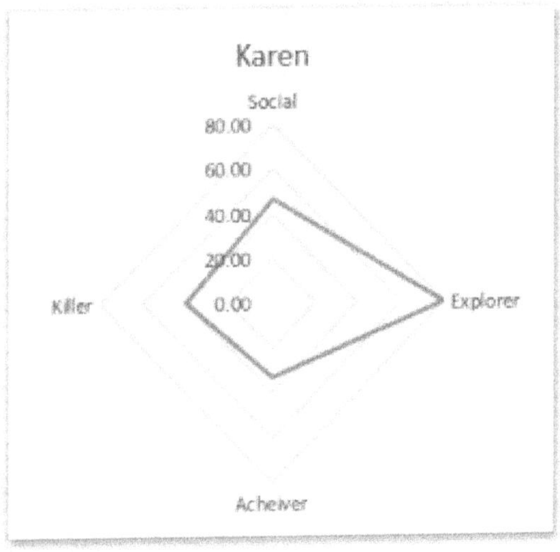

Karen
Social
80.00
60.00
40.00
20.00
0.00
Killer
Explorer
Acheiver

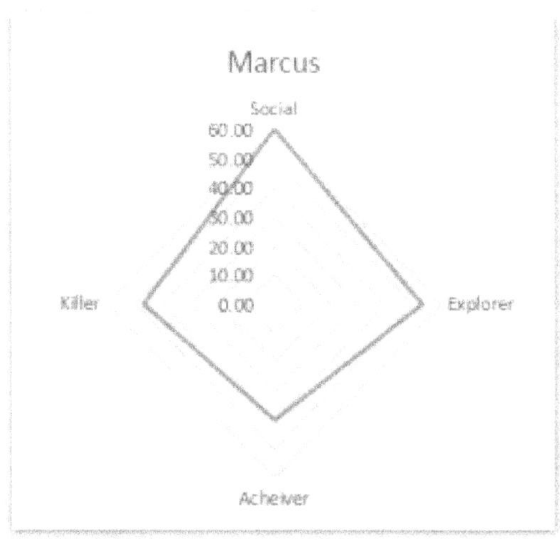
Marcus
Social
60.00
50.00
40.00
30.00
20.00
10.00
0.00
Killer
Explorer
Acheiver

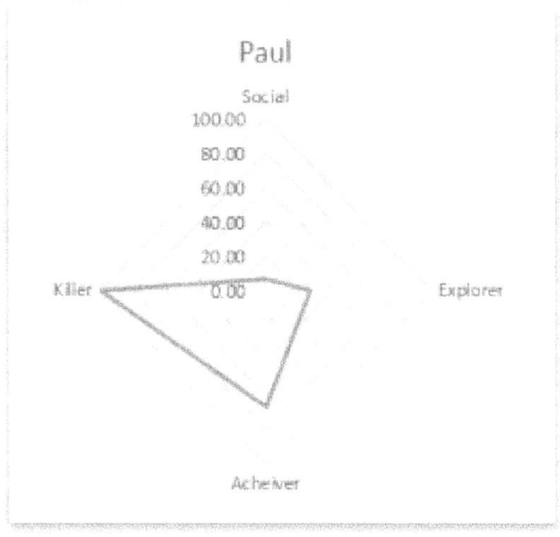
Paul
Social
100.00
80.00
60.00
40.00
20.00
0.00
Killer
Explorer
Acheiver

Determining the Reader's Gaming Type

QUICK AND EASY EDUCATOR Survey

You may have noticed a question about teaching or learning at the end of many chapters. These questions are intended to get you thinking about how your preferred gaming traits might influence your teaching style. If you noted your answers as you read along, skip ahead to the scoring. If you didn't, here are the questions from each chapter so you don't have to go searching back for them:

HOW DO YOU ENCOURAGE creativity in the classroom?

a) Provide clear guidelines and parameters for creative projects

b) Encourage students to think outside the box and experiment with new ideas

c) Encourage collaboration and sharing of ideas

d) Foster a competitive atmosphere that motivates students to be creative

---

HOW DO YOU ENCOURAGE student participation in class?

a) Use a rewards-based system to encourage participation

b) Provide opportunities for hands-on exploration and experimentation

c) Foster a sense of community and belonging in the classroom

d) Create a competitive atmosphere that motivates students to participate

---

HOW DO YOU HANDLE CONFLICTS in the classroom?

a) Apply a set of pre-determined consequences to resolve conflicts

b) Encourage students to express their feelings and work through conflicts together

c) Use conflict as an opportunity to build positive relationships and communication skills

d) Encourage healthy competition and channeling conflicts into competitive challenges

---

FOR WHICH PURPOSE DO you primarily incorporate technology into your teaching?

a) To enhance traditional teaching methods and materials

b) To create new and innovative teaching approaches

c) To facilitate collaboration and communication among students

d) To create competitive games and challenges that test student knowledge

---

HOW DO YOU PREFER TO assess student learning?

a) Traditional tests and assignments that measure their mastery of the material

b) Open-ended projects that allow for creativity and exploration

c) Collaborative group work that emphasizes teamwork and communication

d) Competitive games and challenges that test their skills and knowledge

HOW DO YOU PREFER TO deliver feedback to your students?

a) Constructive criticism and specific areas for improvement

b) Encouragement and praise for creative thinking and exploration

c) Personalized and individualized feedback that addresses their unique needs

d) Friendly competition and recognition for exceptional performance

HOW DO YOU TYPICALLY respond to students who are struggling with material?

a) Provide extra resources and support to help them catch up

b) Encourage them to explore alternative approaches to learning

c) Create opportunities for them to work with and learn from their peers

d) Set up a friendly competition to motivate them to work harder

IN A CLASSROOM SETTING, when are you most engaged?

a) When there are clear objectives and a structured lesson plan

b) When creativity and experimentation is encouraged

c) When someone facilitates group work and discussion

d) When competition or gamification elements are incorporated into the learning

---

WHEN WORKING WITH A group, what are you most likely to do?

a) Take charge and delegate tasks

b) Offer creative ideas and solutions

c) Keep everyone on task and ensure everyone is heard

d) Push for the project to be the best it can be

WHAT DO YOU PREFER to do with your free time?

a) Set goals and work to achieve them

b) Explore new hobbies or interests

c) Spend time with friends and family

d) Play games that involve competition or strategy

WHAT IS YOUR ATTITUDE towards risk-taking in the classroom?

a) Avoid risk-taking and stick to proven methods

b) Encourage students to take risks and try new things

c) Value emotional safety and avoid situations where students may feel uncomfortable

d) Use risk-taking as a motivator and encourage students to embrace challenges

---

WHAT KIND OF PROFESSIONAL development opportunities do you find most engaging?

a) Workshops and training sessions that focus on improving teaching skills and classroom management

b) Conferences and seminars that introduce new and innovative teaching approaches

c) Networking events and opportunities to connect with other educators

d) Competitions and challenges that test teaching skills and knowledge

---

WHEN FACED WITH A DIFFICULT problem, what do you do?

a) Keep working at it until I find a solution

b) Experiment with different solutions and approaches

c) Discuss it with others to get new ideas and perspectives

d) Look for a way to come out on top, even if it means competing with others

---

WHEN GIVEN A NEW TASK, what do you typically do?

a) Break it down into smaller parts and work through it systematically

b) Explore different ways to approach it before settling on one

c) Collaborate with others to brainstorm ideas

d) Find ways to make it more challenging or competitive

WHEN IT COMES TO CLASSROOM management, what is your go-to approach?

a) Create a structured and organized classroom environment

b) Allow for some flexibility and autonomy in student behavior

c) Foster a sense of community and belonging through positive relationships

d) Establish clear rules and consequences for negative behavior

---

WHEN IT COMES TO LESSON planning, what is your primary focus?

a) Ensure that all required material is covered and students are prepared for assessments

b) Provide opportunities for exploration and discovery

c) Create lessons that are engaging and interactive for all students

d) Incorporate friendly competition and challenges into the lesson

---

WHEN LEARNING A NEW subject, what do you find most helpful?

a) Following a structured outline or course

b) Experimenting with different ways to understand the material

c) Discussing the subject with others and collaborating on projects

d) Looking for ways to challenge myself against others in the subject

---

WHAT DO YOU VALUE MOST in a learning environment?

a) Clear objectives and specific goals

b) Opportunities for exploration and experimentation

c) Collaborative work and social connection

d) Challenging materials that push me to excel

WHEN PLANNING A LESSON, what motivates you the most?

a) Seeing my students succeed and achieve their goals

b) Discovering new and innovative ways to teach material

c) Collaborating with other teachers to create an engaging and interactive lesson

d) Competing with myself to make the lesson better than the last

---

WHAT KIND OF GAMES do you most prefer?

a) Ones that have clear objectives and a sense of progression

b) Ones that allow for exploration and discovery

c) Ones that involve playing with friends or meeting new people

d) Ones that are competitive and involve strategy

FOR A FREE PDF COPY of this survey (along with a scoring guide) click here[1].

---

1. https://drive.google.com/file/d/1bgZtTDOgEk5mJWwUeVCyIaOSuXWfj_tA/view?usp=sharing

Incorporating Bartle's gaming styles in lesson planning and teaching can be a powerful tool to engage learners. However, it's important to recognize that our own gaming styles may bias our planning and teaching methods, leading to unintentional exclusion of certain learner types.

How Gaming Styles Bias Teaching Methods

Our own gaming styles can lead to bias in teaching methods. For example, a teacher who identifies as an achiever may unintentionally design lessons that heavily emphasize competition, achievement, and rewards. This approach may not appeal to other gaming types, such as socializers or explorers, who may be more interested in collaboration and exploration. Similarly, a teacher who identifies as a killer may overemphasize competition, leading to an uncomfortable and negative classroom environment for other learners.

Counteracting Gaming Style Biases

To counteract these biases, teachers can start by reflecting on their own gaming style and becoming aware of how it might impact their teaching methods. This can be done through self-reflection or by taking a survey to determine their gaming style. Additionally, teachers can work to incorporate activities and strategies that appeal to different gaming styles, including opportunities for collaboration, exploration, and achievement.

Strategies for Addressing Different Gaming Styles

To appeal to achievers, teachers can provide opportunities for goal-setting, rewards, and competition. To engage socializers, teachers can incorporate group work and community-building activities. Explorers can be engaged through inquiry-based learning and creative problem-solving tasks. Finally, killers can be engaged through healthy competition that is balanced with collaboration and teamwork.

Recognizing our own gaming style biases and working to counteract them can lead to more inclusive and engaging lesson planning and teaching. By incorporating activities and strategies that appeal to different gaming styles, educators can create a classroom environment that is welcoming and engaging for all learners.

The Power of Gaming Types in Education

IN RECENT YEARS, THERE has been a growing interest in using gaming as a tool for learning, and one of the most powerful concepts that has emerged from this area of research is Bartle's gaming types. Bartle's research has identified four main gaming types: achievers, explorers, socializers, and killers. These types can be a powerful tool for teachers when designing their lessons and teaching strategies. By understanding the gaming types of their students, teachers can tailor their lessons to be more engaging and effective.

The impact of using gaming types in education can be significant. By understanding the unique motivations and interests of their students, teachers can design lessons that are more effective and engaging. For example, if a teacher knows that a student is an achiever, they can design lessons that incorporate elements of competition and goal-setting to motivate the student to excel. Similarly, if a teacher knows that a student is an explorer, they can design lessons that incorporate opportunities for discovery and exploration.

Using gaming types in education can also help to promote more inclusive classrooms. By understanding the different gaming types, teachers can better identify and support the needs of all their students. For example, if a teacher knows that a student is a socializer, they can design group activities that allow the student to interact with their peers and build social connections.

Despite the potential benefits of using gaming types in education, there are also some potential drawbacks to be aware of. For example, there is a risk of stereotyping students based on their gaming types, which can lead to a narrow view of their abilities and interests. Additionally, it is important to recognize that not all students fit neatly into one category, and there may be some overlap between the different gaming types.

To address these potential drawbacks, it is important for teachers to approach the use of gaming types with an open mind and a willingness to adapt their strategies as needed. Teachers should avoid labeling their students based solely on their gaming types and should instead use this information as one tool among many for understanding and supporting their students.

Overall, the use of gaming types in teaching has the potential to revolutionize the way we approach education. By understanding the unique motivations and interests of our students, we can design lessons and activities that are more engaging, personalized, and effective. However, it is important to recognize that not all students will fit neatly into one gaming type, and that there may be limitations to using gaming types as a framework for teaching. As such, it is important for educators to continue to explore and refine their understanding of gaming types, and to adapt their teaching strategies accordingly.

Further Reading

BARTLE, RICHARD A. *MMOs from the Inside Out: The History, Design, Fun, and Art of Massively-multiplayer Online Role-playing Games.* Apress, 2015.

Bartle, Richard. *"HEARTS, CLUBS, DIAMONDS, SPADES: PLAYERS WHO SUIT MUDS."* MUSE Ltd, Colchester, Essex, https://mud.co.uk/richard/hcds.htm.

Kapp, Karl. *The Gamification of Learning and Instruction: Game-based Methods and Strategies for Training and Education.* John Wiley & Sons, 2012.

Kapp, Karl, and Lucas Blair. *The Gamification of Learning and Instruction Fieldbook: Ideas into Practice.* John Wiley & Sons, 2013.

Kyatric. "*Bartle's Taxonomy of Player Types and Why It Doesn't Apply to Everything.*" Tuts+ Game Development, Envato Tuts+, 18 Feb. 2013, https://gamedevelopment.tutsplus.com/articles/bartles-taxonomy-of-player-types-and-why-it-doesnt-apply-to-everything—gamedev-4173[1].

Matera, Michael. *Explore Like a Pirate: Engage, Enrich, and Elevate Your Learners with Gamification and Game-inspired Course Design.* Dave Burgess Consulting, Inc., 2015.

---

1. https://gamedevelopment.tutsplus.com/articles/bartles-taxonomy-of-player-types-and-why-it-doesnt-apply-to-everything--gamedev-4173

Don't miss out!

Visit the website below and you can sign up to receive emails whenever Cheryl Angst publishes a new book. There's no charge and no obligation.

https://books2read.com/r/B-A-SBAY-UQGIC

Connecting independent readers to independent writers.

About the Author

Cheryl Angst has been teaching in the classroom for over twenty-five years. With a Masters in curriculum and instruction, her passion centers around finding tips, tricks, and strategies to enhance her practice.

Cheryl is a firm believer that learning should be fun for both the students and the teacher. If it isn't engaging, or doesn't spark joy, it's likely able to be done differently.

The "Quick Reads for Busy Educators" series is designed to maximize the precious time educators have. Each book is short enough to be read in an hour or less, but contains a wealth of information on the topic. Some books are overviews of strategies and approaches (enough to help educators decide if it's for them) and some are deeper dives into specific aspects of those larger approaches. This allows busy educators to grab the information they need quickly and efficiently.

If there's a topic you'd like to see covered in the "Quick Reads" series, please let us know!

www.ingramcontent.com/pod-product-compliance
Lightning Source LLC
Chambersburg PA
CBHW061330120726
48001CB00002B/776